muddy boots

outdoor activities for children

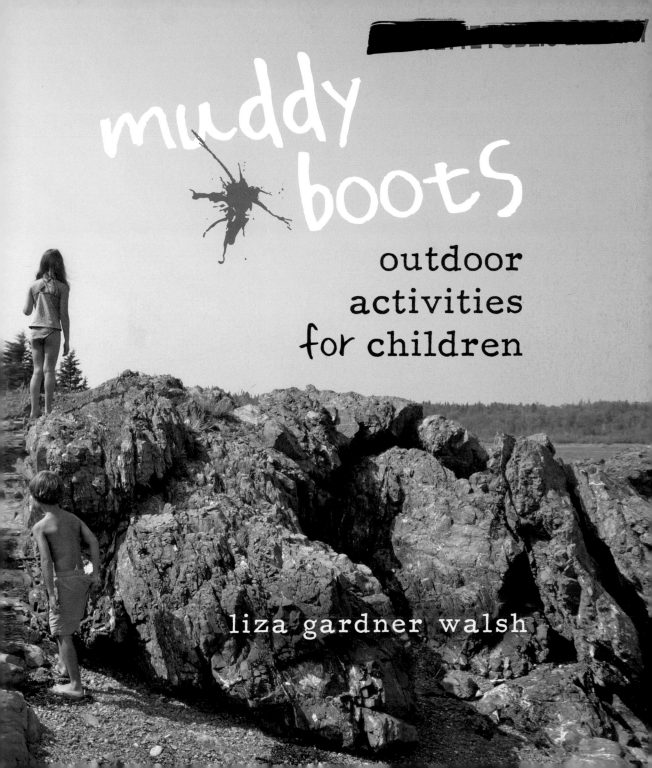

muddy boots

outdoor activities for children

liza gardner walsh

Published by Down East Books
A wholly owned subsidiary of The Rowman & Littlefield Publishing Group, Inc.
4501 Forbes Boulevard, Suite 200, Lanham, MD 20706
www.rowman.com

Unit A, Whitacre Mews, 26-34 Stannary Street, London SE11 4AB

Distributed by NATIONAL BOOK NETWORK

Copyright © 2015 by Liza Gardner Walsh
Designed by Lynda Chilton, Chilton Creative

Photographs © Liza Gardener Walsh, pgs: 9, 13, 15, 21, 25, 26, 27, 28, 29, 30, 31, 32, 33, 36, 39, 42, 43, 44, 45, 52, 53, 58, 59, 60, 62, 64, 65, 66, 68, 69, 73, 80, 81, 87, 89, 90, 91, 97, 101, 111, 122, 123, 125, 127, 130, 131, 136. © Bill Petrini, pgs: 114, all on 115, all on 116, 118, 124. © Lynda Chilton, pg. 51. © Jennifer Mayo Smith, pg. 109. © dreamstime, Muuraa, pg. 1, Alexander Shalaov, pg. 6, Intst, pg, 11, Shawn and Sue Roberts, pg. 16, Anita Patterson Peppers, pg. 18, Pavla Zakova, pg. 37, MNSudio, pg. 40, Natalia Vasilyeva, pg. 44, Greenland, pg. 53, Claruska, pg. 70, Danil Chepko, pg. 84, Waldru, pg. 93, Matt Antonio, pg. 99, Jokerproproduction, pg. 104. © istockphoto: EVAfotografie, pg. 55, CPaulussen, pg. 57, IS_ImageSource, pg. 61, otto549, pg. 63, g215, pg. 72, ParkerDeen, pg. 104. © fotolia Wipahda, pg. 5. © thinkstock, Glenda Powers, pg. 23. © Luc-Henri Fage, pg. 35, © Pudelek, pg. 49, © Mrs Scarborough, pg. 60, © Killy Ridols, pg. 74, © Dbaisley, pg. 77, © John Johnson, pg. 78, © Theymos, pg. 82, © Wikiphoto, pg. 95, © Lumpytrout, pg. 99, © CC BY 2.5, pg. 108, © Fir0002, pg. 113, © Mike's Birds, pg. 119, © Dan Pancamo and Dakota Lynch, pg. 120, © Stemonitis, pg. 121, © Fir0002/Flagstaffotos, pg. 128.

British Library Cataloging in Publication Information Available

Library of Congress Cataloging-in-Publication Data Available

ISBN 978-1-60893-370-9 (cloth : alk. paper)
ISBN 978-1-60893-371-6 (electronic)

♾™ The paper used in this publication meets the minimum requirements of American National Standard for Information Sciences—Permanence of Paper for Printed Library Materials, ANSI/NISO Z39.48-1992.

To Phoebe and Daphne,
who are never afraid to get their
boots muddy!

And to Rachel Carson,
whose remarkable sense of wonder
helped make our world
a better place.

table of contents

A NOTE TO PARENTS

Passion is lifted from the earth itself by the muddy
hands of the young: it travels along grass-stained sleeves
to the heart. If we are going to save the environment,
we must also save the child in nature.

●—— • **Richard Louv**

We all feel it—that sense of panic that our kids' eyes are turning into squares from watching too much television, that they are missing the essential piece of childhood that we had growing up. We can't help comparing the way we spent our youth to the way our kids do. How we were left to our own devices and not to our electronic devices. We sit at playgrounds together and talk about how we never even wanted to be inside, that as soon as the bus dropped us home, we were off on wild adventures. But the reality is that our kids live in a very different world today, and let's face it, we didn't have iPads. Regardless, there is still the wonderful enticement of getting dirty that we remember and want our kids to experience. This book is a reminder of things you probably know, but I hope that by showing them in a different format something might spark for you and

your child. It is a book about getting dirty, getting a little wet, but mostly it is about being engaged. It is about taking simple natural materials and turning them into activities that will hold any kid's attention for more than five minutes—activities that will not only get them dirty but hopefully will pique their curiosity and creativity, allowing them to slow down. Having these experiences together, to wonder at things together, to ask how something happens and then look for answers together, these times are the antidote to that earlier fear I mentioned. Just a few of these experiences will cement a love of the world outside your door. All you need to do to "keep alive [the] inborn sense of wonder without any such gift from the fairies," as Rachel Carson advises, "is to provide the companionship of at least one adult who can share it, rediscovering with them the joy, excitement, and mystery of the world we live in."

Some of you might worry when you see a book called *Muddy Boots* that the mess will be too much to deal with. But heed this advice given to me by my daughter when she was about eight: "Mom, you need to stop cleaning all the time and make some memories." Some of us have inherently high thresholds for chaos and others score very low on the mess-o-meter. But helping kids learn how to get really dirty and then how to clean it up promotes independence and self-care. Plus, there are all those studies now about how dirt is good for the immune system. So go ahead, let them get dirty, and, as authors Jo Schofield and Fiona Danks wisely advise, "Let children become completely immersed in nature. Allow them to get soaked to the skin in a summer rainstorm or plastered from head to foot in mud; let them stain their hands and arms with blackberry juice or have play fights with newly mown grass. Give them the freedom to muck about, get dirty, and generally have fun." And as you let them get dirty and play with this amazing world around us, I hope they will help you reconnect with your younger self. I hope that you will watch your kids and remember the forts you built, the long summer days chasing crickets and fireflies, and again, to cite Rachel Carson, "Exploring nature with your child is largely a matter of becoming receptive to what lies all around you.

It is learning again to use your eyes, ears, nostrils, and finger tips, opening up to the disused channels of sensory impression."

A Word about Safety

I'm all for kids having time to explore the world themselves and learn independence but there are some basics that need to be stressed.

✔ Always have an adult nearby when playing near water.

✔ Never eat berries or leaves, and be very careful to identify poisonous and dangerous plants in your area, especially poison ivy. Consult books and experts, if necessary.

✔ Always wash your hands after playing outside.

✔ Wear insect repellent, long-sleeved shirts and pants when in the woods, and check for ticks.

A NOTE TO KIDS

I meant to do my work today
and a butterfly flitted across the field,
And all the leaves were calling me.
And the wind went sighing over the land,
Tossing the grasses to and fro,
And a rainbow held out its shining hand
So what could I do but laugh and go?

●——• **Richard Le Gallienne**

Guess what? You were born to get dirty. Believe it or not, it is actually one of the most important jobs of being a kid. This book is all about getting dirty and digging deep into nature. It is about asking questions, exploring, and keeping your eyes wide open to the wonder around you. If I meet you after you've read this, I hope your knees will be grass stained and your cheeks will be mud caked; that way I know I will have done my job. Most of you know what to do when you open that door and head out into the great outdoors but, just in case, you have this book. There are ideas in here for mud projects, playing in water and things to do with the many

sticks that cross your path as well as the rocks you kick up on your way to school. But the main thing to remember is that these ideas are just the beginning, and as you play and explore and make your secret hideaways, you will come up with more ideas, and these new ideas will keep you playing outside throughout your life.

Don't worry if you don't live deep in the woods but rather in a big city. There are parks and back-yards everywhere filled to the brim with natural materials. And for many of these activities, you can create your own patches of dirt. As you move along through the book, you will find many different activities, each with a list of ingredients and instructions, making this book a bit like a cookbook. When I cook,

I read the recipe a few times, then figure out what I need. I gather all of my ingredients and step by step I create the meal. Treat these activities like recipes, you can add your own flavors but by following the basic formula you will come up with something cool.

The only thing you must have as you approach these ingredients is curiosity. You don't need fancy outdoor gear. You just need to ask why and what if. Those two questions will guarantee to make your life more interesting. Ask them often. Question constantly. Seek the unknown and seek to know it. For being outside in the world surrounded by fresh air, raindrops, and mud puddles is akin to a laboratory of wonder. Every tree, every bird, every rock, are there to be wondered about. Where is that little bird heading off to? What do they eat? What kind of nest do they build? I encourage you to borrow or buy a magnifying glass and get on your hands and knees to look closely at things. What tiny insects! What amazing crystals in those rocks! The point is that nature is always more than meets the eye, and when you approach it with the sense that I consider one of the most important, that extra sense called wonder, you unlock the door to a lifetime of exploration and discovery. So roll up your sleeves, put on some old clothes, open the door, and let's get muddy.

mud

Mud, mud, I love mud! I m absolutely positively wild about mud. I can t go around it. I ve got to go through it. Beautiful, fabulous, super duper mud.

●—— • **Rick Charette**

What point is there in being a kid if you can t play in the mud?

●—— • **Phoebe Walsh**

dirt is ancient. It's even older than your parents. Humans have created with mud for millions of years, from using it in shelters to creating beautiful works of art such as Malian mud cloth. When you dig in the dirt right outside your door, you are digging through layers of ground-up sediment that has changed through many geological forms. What this means is that by getting dirty, you are connecting to the past, to the earth, and to science. Not to mention that doctors now say getting dirty keeps you healthy. So you have nothing to lose by clomping in a mud puddle or even making some of your own by mixing together good old dirt and water.

There is nothing quite like the feeling of mud coating your bare feet and sliding up through your toes. And there is nothing like that sound—the splunking, sucking, slurping. It's hard to resist taking a bit of that mud in the palm of your hand and forming it into a perfect ball. Or dabbing some on your face, then a little more, so that you start to blend in with the mud. The grownups around you might get frustrated by mud-caked shoes and your white shirt that is now brown, but when they were your age, they did the exact same thing. Anyway, don't worry, I've already given them a pep talk on the basics of mud play and clean up. Plus, all you need to do is head directly into the shower—with your muddy clothes on—to get cleaned up!

This chapter is all about mud. We will cover everything from mud pies to mud monsters. Mud masterpieces will be created. Even a little magic will be made. You know instinctively (that means something you were born knowing) what to do when you come across a big muddy puddle. You stomp through it. You splash, you splish. You stamp your feet up and down. Then you dig in and maybe make a mud pie or two. But what

happens next? This chapter will help you get to that what's next part, so that you and your family can make muddy memories to last a long time.

MUD PIES

Few things in the wonderful world of mud capture the imagination as much as a mud pie. Perhaps because you are combining two of the best words in a kid's vocabulary—mud and pie. The beauty of making mud pies is that it can start simply and be added to over time with elaborate recipes

and kitchen setups. To start all you really need is a good patch of dirt, some water, and some meal ideas—pies, pizza, tacos, muffins, soup. Ask your parents if they have any old kitchen items—empty spice jars, mason jars, rusted muffin tins. If not, see if they can take you to a yard sale or a thrift store, as a little investment in your mud pie kitchen can go a long way. Recyclable containers, such as the bottoms of old milk jugs and plastic salad containers, also work wonders with mud cooking. That is all I will say. I am not going to tell you how to do this, I only want to give you pointers for some of the great things to add to your mud kitchen. Remember that word instinctive, meaning you were born to do this? Well, mud pies, my friend, are every child's birth right. And I have to tell you that some of my favorite dining experiences ever were when my children served me at their mud cafes. Menus were passed out with such items as mud puddle soup, grilled mud sandwiches, grass gumbo, mud loaf, and mud pies à la mode for dessert. Delicious!

If, when you get started, you are hungry for other ideas, you need to check out the best cookbook ever, *Mud Pies and Other Recipes* by Marjorie Winslow. This book is intended as a cookbook for dolls in "kind climates and summertime," and "it is an outdoors cookbook, because dolls dote

on mud, when properly prepared, they love the crunch of pine needles and the sweet feel of seaweed on the tongue." And as she so wisely advises for your mud pie kitchen, "You can use a tree stump for a counter. The sea makes a nice sink; so does a puddle at the end of a hose. For a stove there is the sun, or a flat stone. And ovens are everywhere. You'll find them under bushes, in sandboxes or behind trees."

"Meals" from *Mud Pies and Other Recipes*

Boiled Buttons

This is a hot soup that is simple but simply delicious. Place a handful of buttons in a saucepan half filled with water. Add a pinch of white sand and dust, two fruit tree leaves and a blade of grass for each button. Simmer on a hot rock for a few minutes to bring out the flavor. Ladle into bowls.

Bark Sandwich

Make a buttery mix of dirt, lake water, and pine needles. Heap this on a piece of birch bark and serve.

Back Yard Stew

Mark off a big square in your back yard by walking eight giant steps in each direction. Into a large stewpot put anything you find in this square, such as grass, leaves, stones, twigs, berries, flowers, weeds, and so forth. Season generously with white sand and dust, and add puddle water to cover. The longer this dish stews the better it is.

Some Items for Your Mud-pie Kitchen

Large buckets of water

Smocks

Recipe cards and pencils

Pots, pans, cooking lids

Large metal or plastic bowls

Cooking utensils

Dirt

Pitchers of water

Recycled spice jars: Fill empty spice shakers with toppings such as crushed eggshells, tiny pebbles, sawdust, dried coffee grounds, and crushed dried leaves.

Sifter or colander

Towels and pot holders

MUD SEED BOMBS

Sometimes Mother Nature needs a little help reflowering the world and these seed bombs are the perfect way to lend a hand. As the seeds begin to germinate, the tight ball actually anchors to the ground. In dry areas this is more helpful, as loose seeds tend to blow away or be eaten by birds. Don't forget the most

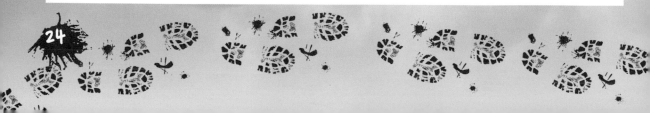

important thing of all about this—making seed bombs is really fun. And they don't have to be shaped like a ball. You can make people, animals—we've even made seed bombs shaped like flower fairies!

Josie Jeffrey discusses some of the benefits of seed bombs in her book, *Seed Bombs: Going Wild with Flowers*. "Seed bombs are full of potential wrapped up in a pocket-sized ball of mud!" says Jeffrey. "They can make ugly, forgotten land beautiful and useful again; restore plant and wildlife populations; nourish and feed the soil, people, and animals; and—importantly—bring joy." The following is a basic recipe for seed bombs (adapted from the website *Gardening Know How* by Jackie Rhoades), but once you have your little balls, feel free to customize. The seeds won't mind one bit!

Materials:

2 parts potting soil

5 parts pottery clay mix from your
    local art store

1-2 parts water

1-2 parts seeds of your choice

Large tub to mix ingredients

Large cardboard box to dry and store
    seed balls

Directions:

Mix the soil, clay, and one part water really well so that you get rid of any lumps. Slowly add more water until the mixture is the consistency of Play-Doh.

Add your collection of seeds; I like using wildflower and butterfly mixes. Knead the dough as if you are making bread and make sure that all the seeds are mixed in. Add more water if needed.

Break off pieces of the mud/clay mixture and roll into balls that are about one inch in diameter. They should hold together easily, and if they start to crumble, simply add more water.

Place seed balls on a tray or cookie sheet and let dry for 24-48 hours in a shady place before sowing or storing. If you do store your seed balls, place them in a cardboard box and not in plastic bags, as they will get moldy.

You are now ready to sow your seed balls. This is the fun part, the part you have been waiting for! Find areas in your yard, on the sides of roads, or in rundown parts of your town and throw your seed bombs out to the world. No need to bury or even water these dynamite little balls, Mother Nature will get right to work on them!

MUD MONSTERS

Once you have mastered the mud pie and the mud seed bomb, you are ready for the wacky and wonderful world of mud monsters, also known as dirt devils, or simply creatures from the dirt. This endeavor combines your hard earned skills of taking mud and shaping it into a perfect ball as well as your sharp eye for collecting good body parts.

All you have to do is start with a simple mud ball and add monster-like features, such as three eyes, a horn, pine needle fur, sticks for claws, shells for super pointy teeth. The whole world is at your creature's finger tips here.

For those gentler souls who prefer animals to monsters or fairies over trolls, you are in luck. Mud hedgehogs make lovely pets, as do mud fairies wrapped in discarded flower petals. Really anyone or anything, monster, person, or animal, can be made from a ball of mud with some sticks for arms and legs.

MUD BRICKS

There is something deeply satisfy-
ing about stacking a pile of bricks
to make a wall. Think Lego, Lincoln
Logs, blocks. Well, guess what?
Bricks are basically dried mud and
you can make a pile of them with-

out too much fuss. Maybe your bricks won't be quite like the ones used
to build the great pyramids in Egypt, but even small bricks can be used to
create little houses for your gnomes, your grasshopper, or even a Lego char-
acter or two. The key for this activity is heat, patience times ten, and a lot
of ice cube trays. If you are an out-of-the-box thinker, shape the bricks by
hand rather than using a form.

Instructions:

Make a batch of mud in a big bucket. Err on the side of drier rather than wetter
mud. You can also add some sand, clay if you have it, or even grass or hay. Mix
everything together with your hands and make sure to work it all in evenly.

Fill each ice cube mold about ¾ of the way with the mud mixture.

Let the trays sit in the sun for a couple of days. If you can remember,
bring them in at night so the humidity and dew won't cancel out all that

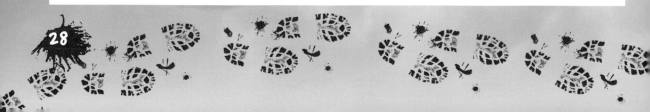

good baking. If you have metal ice cube trays, you can put them in the oven at low temperatures to speed up this process.

After a few days, pop out your little bricks and begin building your mud pyramids, castles, or whatever your imagination decides.

MAGIC MUD

There is no doubt that mud play is magical, but here in this recipe mud actually turns into pure explosive bliss just by adding a couple of simple ingredients. Be careful, as volcanic-sized eruptions have occurred during this activity and they can become habit forming.

Materials:

Dirt

Water

Various cake pans and muffin
     tins, as well as a big plastic
     container

Baking soda

Powdered tempera paints or
     ground-up colored chalk

White vinegar
A 1-cup measuring cup
Assorted spoons

Making the Mud:

Find a good spot outside that has access to water and can be hosed down afterward.

Mix together some dirt and water in a big plastic container. This will be your mud station. You can dig dirt from your yard or just use a bag of potting soil. Slowly mix in water so you get a nice thick mud, a tad thicker than pudding.

Add in a cup or two of baking soda. Using measuring cups, small bowls, or spoons, place the mud into the various containers and tins.

Sprinkle the powdered paint or ground-up colored chalk on top of your mud creations. But don't stir it up too much or the mud will absorb the colors and make them disappear.

Now, for the magic! Slowly pour white vinegar all over the mud. The mud will erupt, as I said earlier, like a volcano and the colors will bubble and explode. Continue adding vinegar and more paint to see how the muddy colors change.

Finally, grab paintbrushes and paper and use your colored, bubbly mud to make art.

MUD PAINTING

Long before paint came in metal tubes that you buy at the art store, early artists used paints mixed with natural materials, most often mud. Ancient artists created mud murals and dirt masterpieces on cave walls, inside their huts, and even on hand woven cloth. Many of us think of mud as brown; well it is, but within that color there are many varieties—light, dark, yellowish, tan. In some areas the dirt has a reddish tinge to it, and in others the soil is as dark as night. With this in mind, look at the dirt around you as if it was an artist's palette and in the following activities you can go ahead and paint the town brown.

Malian Mud Cloth

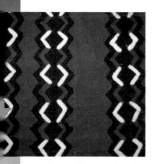

Bogolan cloth

This first mud painting activity is based on an ancient tradition known as Bogolanfini, from the African country of Mali. The process of making traditional Bogolanfini involves numerous steps, including weaving cloth by hand then soaking it in a brown mixture of leaves and water. After drying the cloth in the sun, mud is used to paint intricate geometric designs. The mud is then washed off and the process is repeated until the patterns are dark enough and stand out. The last step is to bleach the non-dyed areas to enhance the contrast.

Make Your Own Malian Mud Cloth

Find an old white T-shirt or a white sheet and set up an outdoor table in an area that won't be bothered by a big mess. Gather some mud or make your own using garden dirt or potting soil and water. You can add black food coloring to darken your mud if you want, but the black food coloring will stain easily, including things other than your mud cloth.

Now it's time to get ready to paint. Have a variety of small and broad brushes on hand to make different designs as well as a big bucket of water for cleaning up as you go.

Characteristic Bogolan cloth uses geometric patterns. Often artists divide their cloth into different sections to make repeating patterns. Others use free standing patterns and geometric shapes and lines. You can do whatever you like as long as you are creative and have fun.

Once the designs are finished, hang the cloth to dry in the sun. Once the mud has set, usually by the end of the day, rinse off the mud to reveal the magical mud stained design.

NOTE: You should hand wash your T-shirt, as machine washing will make the design fade more quickly.

Prehistoric Mud Paint

Another take on mud painting is to recreate the formulas that prehistoric tribes and cave people used to decorate their dwellings. These ancient artists used animal fat, burnt wood, dirt, and groundup rocks for their palette, and many of these paints have lasted for thousands of years. The following recipe does not use animal fat, rather vegetable shortening, which is a little easier to come by. (Adapted from *Nature Smart* by Gwen Diehn, Terry Krautwurst, Alan Anderson, Joe Rhatigan, and Heather Smith)

Materials:

A small shovel
Ziplock bags
A mortar and pestle, or a pie pan and a large spoon or mallet
Vegetable shortening
Small jars, bowls, and cans to store your paint in
A variety of stiff bristled, old, or cheap paint brushes
Thick paper

Take a walk around your neighborhood or yard with your shovel and plastic bags and gather a variety of dirt from different areas—remember dirt from a garden may be a very different color than dirt from a walkway. If you are lucky enough

to have a creek in your neighborhood, look for some natural clay wedged into the banks, and if you happen to have a wood stove or fire pit, you are even luckier because you can add some charcoal to your paint mix! Put each differently colored soil in a separate bag and try to remove any long sticks or small pebbles from your samples.

Pour dirt from one bag into the pie pan or mortar and pestle. Add a spoonful of the shortening and work it together with the soil using the spoon or pestle. Try to get the "paint" as smooth as possible. Add more dirt if the mixture seems too greasy or more shortening if the mixture seems too dry.

Continue to mix up your different samples, adding the ashes or any other variations that you would like. Ideally, you should have a rainbow of brown to begin painting.

You can paint with brushes, a stick, or your own fingers. This paint has the potential to stand the test of time. In fact, you can experiment by painting it on trees, rocks, and other outside areas and see what happens as the days go by.

Make sure you clean up everything! Because of the shortening, this paint will make cleaning the brushes challenging, so you will need to soak them in warm water. And who knows, maybe your kids or grandkids will find remnants of your dirt paintings someday!

MUD SCRATCH ART

Maybe the above activity is too messy and time consuming for you. Maybe you simply want to take the bounty of mud right before your eyes and turn it into a work of art. Well then, this simple activity is right up your alley. All you have to do is paint a piece of wood entirely with mud. While the mud is still wet, use a thin stick to create designs. Go crazy. This is nature's version of scratch art. The beauty of this version is that you can wash it off repeatedly until you have a design you want to keep. When that magic moment happens, just set the mud out in the sun to preserve your masterpiece.

INDOOR MUD

Not every day can be an all-out mud fest. Mudding is a seasonal activity in most parts of the country and sometimes it is just too hot or too cold to be outside. But what if you have a hankering to squish, squeeze, and mush some good old-fashioned mud but the weather isn't cooperating? Well, lucky for you, there are a couple of miraculous indoor mud recipes. Even luckier for your parents is that they are easy and only require a few ingredients.

Indoor Mud Recipe #1

Mix together one large 16-ounce box of baking soda, black watercolor paint or black food coloring, and a bit of water until the texture is mud-like. That's it! Easy peasy. But that's not all . . .

When you are finished playing with this "mud," you can coat plastic dinosaurs with it to make dinosaur eggs. Let the eggs sit and harden for a couple of days, then carve away the outside of the dinosaur egg like a paleontologist looking for fossils.

Indoor Mud Recipe #2

Coffee Play Dough (Adapted from the recipe found on the website *kidsactivitiesblog.com*)

Ingredients:

2 cups of flour

½ cup of coffee grounds

1 tablespoon of instant coffee (if your mud isn't dark enough)

1 cup of salt

2 teaspoons of cream of tartar

1 cup of very hot water

2 tablespoons of oil

Glycerin drops or a tiny shaving from a bar of soap. Glycerin soap bars are the clear or see-through kind.

Mix the dry ingredients. Add the wet ingredients, stir really well, and then let it all sit for a while until it thickens, then stir a little bit more. Presto!

forts

I love the sweet, sequestered place, the gracious roof of gold and green, where arching branches interlace with a glimpse of sky between.

●——• Anonymous

Sometimes you need a place of your own. Maybe your little brother or sister keeps breaking your toys or your older sibling won't let you play with anything at all. Maybe if you stay inside your mom will make you sort all the socks in the laundry or your dad will make you help him clean out the attic. In these times of trouble, a fort is like a lighthouse in a storm.

Look, my friend, you were born with the ability to make yourself a simple fort that gives you a place to escape. A place to hold secret neighborhood meetings. To have picnics, to read, to draw, to think, to plan. What it comes down to is creating a place where you can get away

from it all, a place where you can go to listen to what an amazing woman named Rachel Carson called the "insect orchestra" or the chorus of the birds. A place where you can hear your own thoughts and where you can just be. In the book, *A Kid's Guide to Forts,* author Tom Birdseye says a fort "is a place built using easy-to-find materials, a few tools, and some imagination. It is not made by dad or mom with wood from the lumber company. It is not ordered out of a catalog and delivered by two men in a big truck. It is yours, created by you."

Anyone can build a fort. Think about it—a few walls, a roof, maybe a swept-out floor or one covered with soft pine needles and a moss carpet. But keep in mind, any kind of building requires caution. Wood is by its very nature splintery stuff. Moving big sticks and piles of wood can often result in some bumps and bruises. Anytime sticks are a part of an activity, slow and steady is the required speed. Basically all I am asking is that you pay attention and handle large, sharp objects carefully. Grab a grownup for help when you feel overwhelmed. In this chapter, we will look at making stick dens, igloos, tepees, lean-tos, sunflower houses, and more. But remember that sometimes the best retreats are simply underneath a favorite willow tree or on top of a special lichen-covered rock. I hope you will make

lots of forts and that you will let yourself dream. I hope that in your fort you will catch hold of your deepest wishes and listen to the world around you telling you that you are home.

STICK FORTS — OR LIFE-SIZE FAIRY HOUSES

I love fairy houses—tiny houses in the woods made out of natural materials for the fairies to visit. So I like to think of large stick forts as life-size fairy houses. The same principles apply to both endeavors. You need to find a perfect location to build your fort; a site with a natural element to use as a starting place—a big tree or a huge boulder that can provide support. The site you choose will determine the type of construction. If you are relying on a tree as a wall, you will probably create some sort of a lean-to structure. A free-standing fort will need four strong walls. However you work it, gather your strength, for the next step is to collect your building materials and that means long, straight sticks—lots of them. As you work on these stick houses, try to avoid disturbing the forest floor too much. Many animals and plants live here and aren't crazy about things getting roughed up.

LEAN-TO

Start by leaning your stick poles up against the tree or giant rock so that they rest at an angle. You want to create a wall of sticks, but it's okay if there are slight gaps in the middle. As you lean the sticks, think about where you want to place your entrance to the fort. Weave smaller twigs and stems throughout the framework.

To turn this into a leaf fort, start at the bottom with a big pile of leaves, smooshing them into the sticks. Then work a little higher until the entire structure is coated with leaves. The thicker the wall of leaves, the warmer your leaf hut will be. The result will be a cozy hideaway to keep the autumn chills away.

IGLOOS

Those of you lucky enough to live in wintry wonderlands have perhaps tried to make an igloo before. I apologize if you live in a mild climate, but you should know that for every perfect snowfall there are a dozen sleety days or too-cold days, when not even the bravest snowball makers would venture out. But when the world is covered in enough white for a snow day, Eskimos in training, here is your chance. It's important to be patient when building a snow fort. Snow melts, falls, crumples, and most of all, it is cold. Freezing cold. So a couple of obvious pointers—dress for the cold, take hot-cocoa breaks, and don't expect your snow fort to work perfectly the first time. Enlist a friend, neighbor, or sibling to share in the work and remember to make it small enough that you can reach the higher levels. And one more quick word of caution from my daughter, an igloo master, "it takes longer than you think it will so this is not a good activity for quitters."

All that you need for an igloo is a plastic igloo brick maker or a plastic storage box. Bread loaf pans also work well. In the snow, make a circle for how big you want your igloo to be. Pack your container tightly with snow and then lay your brick by tipping it upside down on the ground. Keep working around until you've laid a circle of snow bricks. For the second layer, place the bricks so they are slightly to the inside of the first layer. Keep laying the bricks for each layer slightly inward of the previous layer. This will give your igloo its dome shape. Pack snow between the cracks as you go and make sure to keep an open area for an entrance. When you finish you can bring blankets out and sit inside your igloo, sipping cocoa to your heart's content.

TEPEES

I think that a tepee is the perfect house. Round, easy to move, easy to build, and nice looking. And once you have the basic formula down, you can build them inside or outside. A tepee can be simple or complex, plain or decorated. There are a lot of variations on how to make a tepee and the following instructions will allow for a pretty large one. To make a smaller version, use about five or six poles instead of the suggested twelve. This is definitely a fort that takes many hands and probably a couple of pairs of grownup hands as well. Not to mention more of that patience I keep talking about.

Andrew Henry's Meadow by Doris Burn

In *Andrew Henry's Meadow,* a frustrated young inventor runs away from home to a quiet meadow because he cannot build anything at his house without annoying his family. In his meadow he builds a house with "walls of clay and rocks and poles. The roof was made of fir boughs, and outside one window there was a fine landing field for dragonflies." But Andrew Henry is not alone for long. Soon, he is joined by other kids who want places of their own, such as Alice Burdock, who loves birds but her father, a farmer, didn't care for them because they ate his crops. And Joe Polasky, who wants an underground house so that his pets, moles, rabbits, and mice, can feel more comfortable. "Soon nine houses stood in the meadow. It looked like a small village." Finally, the children's panicked parents find the meadow. After their fort adventures, the children are ready to go home to houses now willing to tolerate their hobbies.

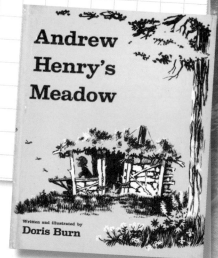

Instructions:

You'll need to gather a bunch of very long straight sticks from the woods a brush pile. Whatever you find, you will need to cut 12 tepee poles 10 feet long and 2 to 3 inches thick at the wide ends.

Lash three poles together with the narrower ends at the top. Do this while the poles are lying on the ground. Then lift them up, spread out the poles so they begin to resemble a pyramid or cone. Continue to add in the other poles to give the tepee extra support.

Once you have completed the framework, you can cover the tepee with old sheets or a painter's drop cloth, or weave vines and branches through it to make a leafy triangle.

SUNFLOWER HOUSE
Adapted from *Sunflower Houses* by Sharon Lovejoy

My summer house is the finest of all with a morning glory roof and sunflower walls.

●——•Sharon Lovejoy

A living, growing, fort that only lasts as long as the warm weather is a pretty magical creation. The beauty of this fort is that you can literally

watch your fort grow day by day. But be forewarned: only after you have tended, watered, and cared for it will it be ready to enter. And when you do part those leafy walls for the first time you will be surrounded by a green hideaway that you grew! Talk about a reward for hard work and patience!

Instructions:

Drag a stick to scratch out a large rectangle that is roughly six feet by nine feet. Dig out a trench a couple of inches deep and plant sunflower seeds and morning glory seeds all along the trench. Water this rectangle every day; water it twice a day if it is hot. Soon you will see little sprouts shooting up around the edge of your plot. Once the flowers get really tall, you might need to stake up some of the plants. When the heads of the sunflower come out, take string and tie the tops of the sunflowers so that they stand up and begin to weave together into a roof.

BEAN TEPEE

This fort is a combination of a tepee and a sunflower house mixed with a side of vegetables! Bean plants are very rapid climbers and need something to lean on as they climb. Take advantage of their clingy vines by making a bean filled hideaway. Set four to six poles in the ground. Bring them together to form a tepee shape. Plant scarlet runner beans in a circle around the base of the tepee. The plants will climb the tepee and you can sit inside in the shade and eat beans all summer long! The added bonus is that your parents will be so happy with all of the veggies you are eating, you might get dessert!

sticks and stones

Y ou probably already know this, but there are things right outside your door that will give you more hours of unlimited entertainment than anything in your toy box. I'm talking about sticks and stones. Sure, there is the old expression, "sticks and stones will break your bones," but I promise that what you can do with a couple of sticks, some flat rocks, and a free afternoon will challenge any computer game. Amazingly, the earth gives you all this stuff to play with for free, with no chemicals added and nothing made in a factory. You don't even need a car to go pick it up. All you need is an eager mind, a bit of time, and some energy—things I am sure you have loads of!

I will cover the nuts and bolts, or rather the sticks and stones of playing with these elementary toy things. Rocks will be balanced, arranged, and used for time pieces. Sticks will be transformed into creatures, brooms, and looms. All you have to do is add your colorful imagination, add new twists, and new colors. Make them your own. And most importantly, have fun.

A word of caution: There's one big, big, important rule when it comes to playing with sticks: NO RUNNING WITH STICKS!!! PERIOD. It is a hard

one to remember in the midst of a stick fest but it is very important. There is another rule that has more to do with the health of the world than the health of you: Be gentle with nature. Always collect your sticks from the ground. There is no need to EVER pull a branch off a living tree for any of these activities. Trees are living things and deserve our deepest respect, so gather your sticks with care.

TINY TWIG RAFTS

Think of the following activity as advanced training in basic boat building or preparation in case you ever get stranded on a deserted island. Just kidding. Making little boats is the ultimate in having an adventurous and creative afternoon on the water. Tiny twig rafts can be made either with or without glue, but either way you will have a lovely little vessel for small creatures or your imagination to sail away on.

Materials:

Twigs

Wood glue

Twine

Scissors

Gather nine to twelve twigs that are as wide around as your finger or a pencil. They all need to be roughly the same size and length, so you may need to break them off to the right length. Try to find straight sticks without too many curves or rough edges.

Lay two of the twigs down horizontally as a base to set the other sticks on. They should be about as far apart as the length of your twigs. Slather these two sticks with glue and place all of the remaining sticks in a row on top of the two bases so they are aligned with the two ends of your sticks.

If you want a more complicated project or a more naturally inspired one, forgo the glue and use twine instead to weave around each stick as well as the base sticks.

Once the glue has dried on your raft or you have finished weaving it, it is a good idea to tie another long piece of twine so that your vessel won't float away when you take it for your first sail. First test how your boat floats in shallow water. If it seems to stay on top of the water let it go and watch it float downstream.

This is an activity made for groups. It is always interesting to see how different everyone's boat looks despite using the same materials. Once everyone has built their boats, test them out and see whose is the fastest and whose stays together the longest. You can even have a twig boat regatta with prizes.

To make your boat even more stable, faster, and more seaworthy, attach some kind of a keel or a weight, such as a thin rock, underneath the boat so that it doesn't tip over as easily, or add a sail by wedging a taller stick in the center and attaching a triangle shaped piece of fabric. Ahoy!

PAINTING WITH STICKS

Berry Ink and Stick Pen

Long before you had a pencil box filled with nice yellow pencils, people used sticks for writing. Sharpened sticks are the great grandparents of the pencil so in this activity we are going to travel back in time a little. Some of you might be comfortable whittling, but since it involves knives, this is definitely an activity that needs a parent around. Find a stick as thin as a regular pencil and ask your parent to help you sharpen the end into a fine point. Crush a bunch of raspberries, blueberries, or blackberries with some water to make a very authentic berry ink. Dip your writing stick into the ink, grab some paper, and write away! The best thing about this ink is that if you make a mistake or the ink spills, you can lick it up. Edible ink!

Stick Brushes

Once you have created a stick pencil, you can move up to a stick paint brush. You will need the same type of stick as your pencil, but the bristles are made from a whole range of materials, such as feathers, pine needles, pussy willows, or evergreen branches. Each variety of

bristles will create different texture in your painting.

To attach the selected bristles (for example, feathers), place the tips at the base of your stick, then wrap a small piece of pipe cleaner or thin wire around the tips of the feathers, and the base of the stick many times so that it is secure. Take note of how each brush stroke differs and how each texture makes distinct features in your painting.

Charcoal Stick Pencils

This activity is the trickiest of all because it absolutely requires an adult's help. Find the same kind of pencil-shaped stick you have been working with and ask a grownup to hold it in a fire for a few minutes until it catches and the end is burned black. Dip the tip in a cup of water to make sure there is no spark whatsoever. Voila—you will have a lovely charcoal pencil to draw with, and as an added bonus this type of pencil works on rocks and wood as well as paper.

NATURE WEAVING

Not only are sticks great for boats and pens but they are also perfect for making wild weaving looms. Wild weaving is a type of weaving that can change through the seasons as you weave in all kinds of different plants and vines. In the summer you can gather wildflowers and leafy vines; and in the fall you can weave with golden vines and autumn leaves. Find a strong, healthy stick with a nice fork in it. Take some string or yarn and wrap it across the width of the fork. Keep wrapping until the length of the fork is covered with lines of string. Then gather a variety of natural materials and weave them through.

This activity can be adapted in many ways. You

can make a square stick loom by lashing four sticks together to form a frame. Then loop your yarn or string around the frame. Or you can make a plywood frame like the one at left that can be a permanent fixture in your backyard.

STICK PEEPS

At my daughter's school, they have an old tradition of going to a nearby nature center and creating what they call "Peeps." These are stick characters that use natural materials for clothing, hair, and accessories. It is amazing what some pine needle hair, berry eyes, and mossy skirts can do to a stick!

To make your very own Peep, gather a forked stick that is about a foot long, the fork of the stick will be the legs. Find a smaller stick that will become the arms of your Peep. Using a piece of twine, lash the arm stick in place across the body of the Peep.

Now gather lots of materials to make a head, clothes, eyes, a mouth, hair, a hat, and any other accessories that you can imagine. Using a glue gun or some tacky glue, attach your natural clothing so that your Peep won't be cold or, even worse, naked.

You can also use a bit of clay to make a head for your stick person. Clay has the advantage of being easy for stuff to stick to—such as pine needles for hair or pebbles for eyes—all touches that will make your stick person unique and lifelike.

PAINTED WALKING STICKS

Having a walking stick for a family hike is a great way to keep your stride and stay balanced on rocky terrain. But the best part is actually at the beginning—finding a stick that's just right for you. The one that is not too tall or too bendy but that fits your hand and helps you with each uphill step. To make this stick even more special, once the hike is over bring it home and add some paint. The sky is the limit on how you make it look, but the following activity is one way to get your stick in style for the next hike.

Materials:

Masking tape

Your just-right stick

Paint

Brush

Wrap your stick with several bands of masking tape. The bands can be close together or far apart. You can make a distinct pattern or keep it simple with random stripes. Prepare your paint palette with a bunch of bright colors and then paint the stick different colors or patterns in between the masking tape. Wait for several hours before removing your tape, or at least until the paint feels dry to the touch. Peel off your tape and reveal your colorful walking stick all ready for adventure!

For another colorful walking stick project, try wrapping your stick with brightly colored yarn which has the added bonus of making an extra soft place for your hand.

SCAVENGING STICKS

A scavenging stick is a stick that tells a story of your wild adventures. It is a stick that allows all of the treasures you have found to be displayed and used for magic or storytelling. Shamans, indigenous healers, use a version of scavenging sticks as they tell healing stories to the people in their tribes. Many native tribes use decorated sticks to recollect journeys and heroic hunts and battles. All you need to do for this activity is find a stick that calls to you—one with a lot of personality—perhaps with a nice curve in it or lots of bumps. Once you find this magical stick, start to gather feathers, special stones, leaves, and other items from your natural collections. Attach them all with twine or wire, or you can simply hang your treasure off the end of your stick with colorful yarn. Don't forget to pull your stick out anytime magic is needed or a special gathering of friends is taking place. Maybe your stick can be the keeper of stories in the special fort you made out of the other sticks you've collected. Whatever you use it for, you can always add to your scavenging stick as each new treasure comes your way.

ROCKS

When you hold a rock, you are holding something that has a long story, something that is as old as the hills. And there are millions of them, all different kinds of rocks. Some are brightly colored, some are hard, and others are fragile, but they are sitting there waiting for you to discover them. You can write with chalky rocks, carve with hard, pointy rocks, skip them, stack them, and collect them. But please, promise me you won't ever throw

a rock at anyone. Rocks, as I just mentioned, are hard. They can really hurt. So if you are ever tempted to chuck one, which is a normal temptation, pause, look around and make sure no one is in range. Then get right back to collecting and creating.

SUN CLOCK

This is an activity that uses both rocks and sticks to tell time the way people did before clocks and wristwatches. This activity takes a bit of stick-to-it-iv-ness, as you'll need to tend to your sun clock each hour. You will want to have a watch on hand to make sure things are set up the right way but once you get the hang of it, you can put away the modern technology and rely purely on the sun! Another perk to this activity is the that knowledge gained will also help in determining meal times so you won't

have to ask that dreaded question to your parents, "When is lunch?" All you have to do is look up. When the sun is directly overhead, head in for a peanut butter and jelly. When it falls slightly lower, time for a cookie. Even lower, you guessed it—dinner!

Materials:

One long straight stick, about a foot long

Twelve small rocks

A watch

Drive your straight stick directly into the dirt in a clear spot that receives sun all day long. A backyard or even a beach work well. Make sure you set your stick in a place where no one will move your clock. Each hour, take one of the rocks and set it where the shadow of the stick falls. At noon, the stick will not create a shadow because the sun is directly over-head. In the morning, one side of the stick will be shaded, and in the after-noon, the opposite side will be shaded. By the end of the day, you will have a straight line of rocks marking each hour of the day. No ding dong or tick tock needed!

ROCKY BEACH ART

Not every beach is filled with soft sand; in fact, many are filled with pebbles and rocks galore. One of the best things about a rocky beach is making a variety of rock creations. Finding those perfect beach stones is a little like looking for your just right stick. Certain ones call out to you because of their color and shape. But the beauty of making rock art is that you can combine all of your finds to create magnificent stone structures, even making an entire village out of pebbles. Stack little stones up to make walls and then create pebble gardens and playgrounds. Build towers to protect your village and plant seaweed trees in the gardens and village

squares. But that is not all—you can make large chairs and tables for sea nymphs and mermaids to come ashore and rest their weary sea bones in. Another fun activity is to create pebble patterns by finding groups of stones that are different colors and sorting them into spirals with dark and light colored stones. Or make an outline of a picture and fill it with different shades of stone.

STONE TOWER GAME

If you and your family and friends are at a particularly rocky spot, you can play the classic rock tower game. The challenge is to see who can make the highest tower before it falls down. Be forewarned, care needs to be taken with this activity, for when it tumbles it could fall on you and that would hurt quite a lot. The key is to start your tower on a big, broad base. As it rises, choose smaller rocks with each level. In the spirit of leave no trace, it is a good idea to enjoy your tower while you're at the beach but break it down when you leave so as not to change the landscape.

SKIPPING ROCKS

Skipping rocks is a skill that can take a while to master. But who knows, maybe you will get it the first time and easily beat the Guinness World Record of fifty-one skips in one throw. If you are anything like me, your skipping arm will take some time to develop but the hard work will no doubt be worth it.

The first and most important step is to select your rock. Look for a thin, flat, round rock roughly the size of your palm. The flatter the stone, the better it will skip across the surface of the water.

Place your index finger on the outer edge of the rock and hold the flat sides of the rock with your thumb on one side and your middle finger on

Roxaboxen by Alice McLerran and illustrated by Barbara Cooney

One of my favorite all-time books is called *Roxaboxen*. This book talks about an imaginary childhood town that the author created when she and her friends were young. "Marian called it Roxaboxen. (She always knew the name of everything.) There across the road, it looked like any rocky hill—nothing but sand and rocks, some old wooden boxes, cactus and greasewood and thorny ocotillo—but it was a special place." One day, Marian digs up a box of black pebbles and everyone knows it is a buried treasure and soon pebbles became the money of the town. As the town grew, rocks were used to outline all of the houses and streets of the town. "Main Street first, edged with the whitest ones, and then the houses. Charles made his out of the biggest stones. After all, he was the oldest." In this rock-lined town, there was a town hall and a mayor, of course, and sometimes even wars. And "because everyone had plenty of money, there were plenty of shops." There was even a jail and a graveyard for a dead lizard. And even as the kids grew older, none of them ever forgot the magic of Roxaboxen. Fifty years later, Frances went back and Roxaboxen was still there. "She could see the white stones bordering Main Street, and there where she had built her house."

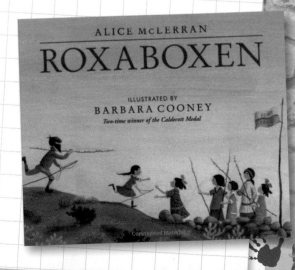

the other so that they are almost pinching the rock. Turn sideways with your shoulder turned toward the water and place your feet shoulder-width apart. Bend down toward the water so that when you throw, your rock will skim the top surface of the water.

Bend your wrist all the way back and flick the rock. Snap. Not like a Frisbee throw but more like you are throwing a baseball underhand. And just like baseball, follow through as you throw. A solid follow through will allow your skip to travel the furthest and bounce on top of the water— maybe even fifty-one times like the Guinness Record I mentioned before!

ROCK CAIRNS

Perhaps on a hike, you have stumbled upon a big triangular-shaped pile of rocks marking a point in the trail where there are several ways to go. This tower of rocks is called a cairn, a stone pile that marks a path. Sometimes hikers create cairns in very rocky parts of a trail to create a monument to the fact that they have made it to a high point and so they are leaving a mark. You can think of it as a guest book made out of stones. Others make cairns at a tricky point in a trail when it seems like there could be more than one way to go. Not everyone approves of this activity because it changes the natural landscape and can damage delicate mountain plant and animal habitats.

But recognizing them and taking a shot at building one while in a rocky spot can also be fun. You can certainly break your cairn down after you build it if you are in a natural area, and you can make more permanent ones around your yard.

An interesting tradition of stone sculptures occurs in the Arctic, where Inuit tribes build cairns that serve more purposes than marking the way. These structures are called *Inukshuk,* which means "in the likeness of a human." According to author Norman Hallendy, who wrote a book called *Inuksuit: The Silent Messengers,* "The Inuit make inukshuk in different forms for a variety of purposes: as navigational aids, to mark a place of respect or memorial for a beloved

person, or to indicate migration routes or places where fish can be found. Other similar stone structures signify places of power or the houses of spirits." You can make your own version of an Inukshuk and create a stone

tower in the shape of a human by finding rocks shaped like various body parts and assembling them. Perhaps you can even make your whole family, including your dogs and cats. Maybe even your pet gerbil.

PAINTED ROCKS

Rocks, other than being a great thing to collect, stack, and skip, can be a perfect artist's canvas. Paint practically glides onto the surface of a nice flat rock. Painting a rock collection is a great thing to do on a rainy day and painted rocks make great paper weights and gifts for your teacher. The following activities are just a few of the many creative rock painting ideas out there.

LETTER ROCKS

Collect a bunch of small round stones, at least twenty-six but probably more like thirty so you can have extra vowels. Write the alphabet with a permanent marker, adding a few extra a's, o's, i's, u's, and e's. This is a great way to practice spelling with younger friends as well as planting words in certain places. For example, you can spell out words like "candy" and "new toy" and put them in places that your parents see every day.

STORY STONES

Story stones are a collection of stones painted with key story elements on them, such as a fire, a barn, a pig, or an alien. The more pictures you paint, the more elaborate your story will be. Combining each picture will allow you to tell a unique story each time that you play with the stones. For example, there was once a pig that lived in a barn. One day, there was a huge fire and an alien landed on the burnt barn and became friends with the pig. Okay, maybe that isn't the best example, but you get the idea.

Face Rocks: Similar to story stones, face rocks are rocks that have different facial features painted on them. You can paint human-like features, eyes, ears, noses, but you can also make snouts, or lizard's tongues, or a kitten's nose. Place the various features together to make wacky and wonderful faces framed with pebble hair.

ANIMAL ROCKS, ALSO KNOWN AS PET ROCKS

Certain rocks might call out to you to be painted like an animal or a critter. You can make anything your heart desires, including bumblebees, lady bugs, or turtles. The choice is largely based on the type of rocks you discover, as some look like a body of a bear while others look like the neck of a giraffe. You might decide to make multi-dimensional animals by using several rocks and gluing them together or just paint a smooth oval rock to look like a turtle shell. To really make the animal come out in your rock creation, you can glue on wiggly eyes so that your animal can find its way home.

water

Rain! Whose soft architectural hands have power to cut stones, and chisel to shapes of grandeur the very mountains.

A Henry Ward Beecher

Then all the needles on the evergreens wear a sheath of silver; , ferns seem to have grown to almost tropical lushness, and every leaf has its edging of crystal drops. Now I know that for children, too, nature reserves some of her choice rewards for days when her mood appears to be somber.

Rachel Carson

do you know anyone who can resist walking smack dab into a puddle? I don't. This chapter is a call for puddle jumpers to unite and celebrate all of that soggy joy! Water in general is all around magical—rain, lakes, rivers, ocean, the hose, the faucet, and even the bathtub. It's splishy and splashy, cools you down, cleans you, and quenches your thirst.

Not to mention the music—the sound of a river gurgling by, waves lapping on the shore, drops of rain on your roof as you fall asleep. There is a reason why Earth is often called the blue planet: because so much of it is covered with water. It's everywhere. In this chapter we will make our own rivers, dams, and boats. We will put on our boots and dance in the rain as well as use it to make art. So grab a rain coat or a bathing suit, and perhaps an umbrella, and get ready for some wet and wild fun.

Safety Tips:

✔ Always have a grownup nearby when playing near water.

✔ Wet clothes get cold fast, so either pack an extra set of clothes or run inside and change before you get too cold.

✔ Be careful if you're barefoot in puddles. There might be something sharp at the bottom that you can't easily see.

✔ Avoid splashing water in people's faces. It is rude, bothersome, and makes water play not as much fun.

✔ Also, remember that water is precious. Try to think about conserving water as you play. Do not leave the hose on for any longer than is necessary and try to reuse your play water to water the plants in your garden.

PUDDLE SCIENCE

After a big rain, hopefully your park, driveway, or sidewalk will be filled with delightful, tempting puddles. With your rain boots on you absolutely must jump in and clomp about. Pay attention to all of the sounds you make as you stomp around. Splash that rain water and then let it settle completely. Now what? Look deeply at this puddle and begin to ask some questions. Become a puddle scientist. Gather some pebbles, leaves, flowers, pine needles, and other natural materials. Start throwing them into the puddle one by one. Why do some things float and other items sink? This is called flotation.

How deep is your puddle? Grab a stick and poke it into the center of your puddle until it stops at the bottom. Measure the wet line to determine the depth.

Watch your puddle throughout the day to see if it gets smaller. Sadly, puddles will evaporate and vanish until the next big rain, so all you can do is take advantage of a puddle while that wet wonder is right before your eyes and feet.

RAIN PAINTING

This activity is not something you can do every day and will require you to do a little bit of weather forecasting. On a rainy day or even on a day before you know it's going to rain, gather your rain painting materials: paper,

watercolors, and a paint brush. Take a large piece of paper and cover the entire surface with watercolor paint. You can paint it one color or many different colors. You can make a design; draw a face, or a landscape —whatever you want. Then let your watercolor dry completely.

Once the rain is coming down, bring your painting outside and let the raindrops splash onto it, creating a new effect. The drops of rain will create a new pattern on your watercolor. Repeat as necessary until you get something you really like. When I did this activity with some young friends at Peopleplace Cooperative Preschool, I asked them what they thought might happen. Here is what they said:

Sam: I think it might turn bubbly.

Rowan: It might turn into a butterfly.

Sam: Why do you think it will turn into a butterfly?

Rowan: I don't know? I haven't done this before. But I have jumped off the bench at my old house.

Sam: I can't wait to see what happens.

Rowan: We don't know, do we?

RIVER MAKING

Adapted from *River Wild* by Nancy Castaldo

If you've ever stood next to a river, you probably noticed a few things right away, mainly where the river sped up and slowed down. If you visit another river, you will quickly notice that it is different than the last one and that no two rivers are exactly alike. The following activity allows you to pretend you are the giant river maker and at the same time shows how rivers are formed and what they do to the land as they move merrily along.

Materials:

A plastic tarp

2 buckets of sand

A bucket of fist-sized rocks

1 bucket of mud

A pitcher of water

What to do:

Spread your tarp on the ground. Since many rivers begin their lives on mountaintops, your rocks are going to become a mountain. Pile them into a cone shape on one side of the tarp.

Coat the rocks with mud and sand to fill in all of the cracks in between the rocks. Add mud and sand to the bottom of the mountain.

Slowly pour the water from your pitcher over the mountain and watch carefully to see the path it takes. Does the water take one or two paths down your mountainside? Does the water widen as it comes to the bottom of the mountain? Does any of the sand and mud join the water on its way downstream?

Now make a dam and see what happens to the river. Gather a handful of small twigs about six inches long each. Tie them all together with twine or bind them with pipe cleaners so they form a rectangle. Put the dam near the bottom of the mountain and try pouring another pitcher of water over your mountain again. Does a lake form?

If you live on a hill, use your dam the next time it rains to see if you can create a rain river. You can also make rivers in your sand box or at the beach by digging trenches and letting water pour through.

BIRCH BARK CANOES
Adapted from *Nature Smart* by Gwen Diehn, Terry Krautwurst, Alan Anderson, Joe Rhatigan, and Heather Smith

Tired though he was, he climbed a spruce tree and found some spruce gum. With this he plugged the seam and stopped the leak. Even so, the canoe turned out to be a cranky little craft. If Stuart had not plenty of experience on the water, he would have got into serious trouble with it.

● — • **E. B. White, *Stuart Little***

Native tribes made birch bark canoes that roamed the waterways of this country. To make a real birch bark canoe is a very time consuming process, but miniature ones can be created in just a couple of hours. To make your canoe really water tight, you might need to coat it with a little furniture wax or, if you are brave like Stuart Little, you can use sap from a tree.

Materials:

A piece of birch bark, gathered from the ground, not ripped off of a tree (never pull bark off a living tree; it is very bad for the tree). The piece should be about 4 to 5 inches wide and a foot long.

A large needle

Raffia

A hole punch

2 clothespins

A glue gun

Paper and pencil

A bowl of warm water

Sharp scissors

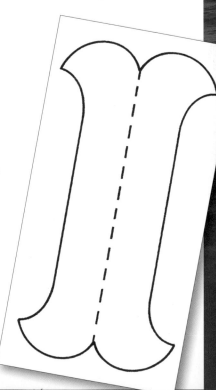

On a piece of paper, make a pattern for your canoe. Cut it out and trace it onto the back side of your bark. Cut out the canoe shape.

Soak the bark in the bowl with warm water to soften it before you prepare to bend it and sew it together.

Fold the sides together and use the clothespins to hold it together until the bark dries out.

With help from an adult, hot glue the corners of the canoe together. Re-attach the clothespins over the glued areas until the glue dries and the canoe shape holds.

Use the hole punch to punch holes along the sides of the canoe. Thread the needle and sew raffia through these holes to create a laced pattern.

Set your canoe in the water and see if it floats. Remember, it might not be completely water tight, so you can experiment with different ways to seal it. Think of Stuart Little and imagine the other little creatures who might take your canoe for a turn.

FAIRY BOATS

Making little boats provides hours of entertainment and allows for lots of creativity, especially when you are creating a special boat out of acorn caps, twigs, leaves, bark, and other natural materials for the fairies to set sail on. Fairy boats can be made by simply gathering up all of these bits of nature tucked around your yard or garden or

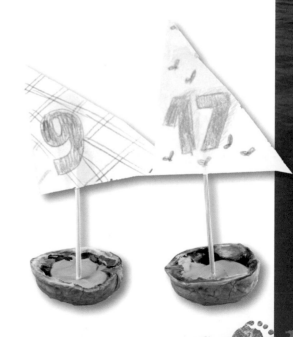

forest. Truly the process of making fairy boats is as free and wide open as fairies are themselves. You can make a simple boat out of a big, wide leaf or a more sturdy type with bark and a stick for a mast and a leaf sail. To fasten the bits of your boat together, you can use clay, mud, or twine. Flowers are lovely decorations for your boats, as well as small berries and even tiny sea shells. And once you have made a fairy boat fleet, you can test them all by bringing them to a stream or body of water nearby, but even a bath tub will work!

ACORN CAP BOATS

Acorn caps have a myriad of uses in nature play. They can be bowls for fairies and frogs; they can be hats for grasshoppers and gnomes. But in the following activity, those tiny caps are filled with a bit of wax to create a magical activity that will help make your dreams come true!

Materials:

Acorn caps

Beeswax

Wicks

Cut a half-inch piece of candle wick and set it in the center of an acorn cap. Have a grownup help you melt a small amount of beeswax in a double boiler. Have an adult pour a tiny amount into an acorn cap so that is almost filled up. This will be very hot. Make sure the wick is not covered by the wax. Let the wax dry for several hours. Later that night set your acorn cap candle boat to float in a big bowl of water. Have a grownup light the candle and watch as it floats along. When you are ready, close your eyes and make a wish.

You can also make acorn cap boats that don't have a candle. Put a tiny piece of clay in the center of an acorn and stick half of a tooth pick in the center. Take a tiny paper or fabric triangle and decorate it into a sail. Using tape, attach your sail to the toothpick. Leaves and flowers also serve as sails, making more of a natural looking tiny boat.

WATER WONDER WATCHER

In any small pond, brook, or shallow lake, a whole world exists right under the surface. Tadpoles, baby fish, and water bugs frolic beneath the ripples just below sight. With this cool, yet simple water viewer, you will get a glimpse of them without having to put on your bathing suit and goggles.

Materials:

A milk carton
Plastic wrap
Large rubber band or duct tape
Scissors

Cut away the top half of an old milk carton. Make sure you wash it out really well so it doesn't smell like sour milk. Cut out a smaller square on the bottom of the milk carton. Take the plastic wrap and place it over the opening. Make sure it fits snugly over the top. Then take your rubber band or duct tape and secure the plastic wrap. This is the underwater viewer part of your contraption. Place this end in the water to see all the wonders that lie beneath.

BE SAFE: Only do these activities in still, shallow water. Do not wade above your knees and stay out of any fast water completely. And make sure your parents or another adult relative are with you. Children need to be very well supervised when playing near rivers and ponds.

ICE ORBS AND LANTERNS

For those of you in cold climates, you have the fortune of watching as the ponds you swam in over the summer become the ponds you skate on. Perhaps you've seen icicles hanging from your roof and window sills. Or hopped on frozen puddles to see them crack apart. The following activities are just a few of the many cool things you can do when the weather cools and your water play changes into ice play.

ICE ORBS

These brightly colored frozen balls brighten up a white landscape. For this activity you will need balloons, food coloring, water, and either a really big freezer or cold temperatures. You simply fill the balloon up with water, trying your hardest not to have a water balloon fight, and add one of the food colors. You don't need more than four or five drops to make a strong color. For each balloon add a different color so that you get a nice rainbow effect. Then tie the balloon tightly and set it out in the freezing temperatures or in a large freezer. When the balloons have frozen solid, cut away the balloon (although the material might have already cracked) and you will have a beautiful orb of colored ice to decorate your wintery world.

ICE LANTERNS
Adapted from *Instructables.com*

In our town, we actually have amazing ice lantern fairies who every winter make a dozen or so lanterns and light them each night so our streets glow with a magic crystal light. Making your own ice lanterns is a great activity for Winter Solstice parties or any kind of winter gathering. And the beauty is that they will stay around as long as the cold weather does.

How to:

Find a bucket or several. Regular household buckets work well. Fill them with cold water but leave at least one inch so the ice can expand. Next bring the buckets outside in the freezing temperatures. Let the water freeze but not completely. This is tricky but usually a full day will be enough. You want to have at least two inches of frozen water on the top.

The sides and the top will be frozen but the center will still have water. To get the lantern out, tip it upside down and pour a small amount of hot water over the bucket. The ice should make a loud slurping sound as it releases itself. This is a sensitive part of the process because the lantern can be fragile. There should be water in the center so make a small crack in the top to pour out the remaining cold water. At this point, you can also check to see if there are any cracks and if there are you can pour some water over the lantern and it will begin to freeze them together.

Find the spot where you would like to set the lantern. There will be a hollow center where you can stick a candle inside and the tall walls will keep the candle burning bright throughout the frigid and windy winter nights.

explore, create, repeat

Hurt no living thing:
Ladybird, nor butterfly,
Nor moth with dusty wing,
Nor cricket chirping cheerily,
Nor grasshopper so light of leap,
Nor dancing gnat, nor beetle fat,
Nor harmless worms that creep.

●——• **Christina Rosetti**

You have officially gotten your boots muddy. You have waded in the water, made boats, stacked rocks, created stick art, and built secret hideouts. Can there be anything more? You know as well as I do that the world outside your door is limitless, that there is no point when the wonders of the world stop surprising you. So here we are at the part of the book where we talk about exploring. About using your two eyes and taking stock of all the amazing things around you. The spot where we talk about opening your ears and listening to the birds, bugs, and bees. See, one day, you will find an animal track that you have never seen and will ask yourself if is it a bobcat or a raccoon? And then the next day, you might listen for a bird song that sounds like someone saying, "how dee do dee," and you will have to race back to your sources to identify it. This kind of work can keep you busy for the rest of your life. In fact, birders keep a list of the birds they have seen called a life list. I like to make a life list that includes more than birds. Mine has things like saw a shooting star, swam with phosphorescence, found a snake skin. So my first advice is to get a nature notebook. Keep track of the amazing things that you discover. Make a life list. Sketch the views from mountains and shorelines. Make lists of bugs you know. Rocks. Trees. Flowers. Be an avid watcher. Pay attention. This world is filled to the brim with things to see and to take note of. Enjoy. Explore. Create. Repeat.

How to use crickets as a thermometer

In summer, the sound of crickets is everywhere. Who knew that by counting chirps and doing a little math you could predict how hot it is outside? All you need to do is count the number of times a cricket chirps in fourteen seconds. Add forty to this number and you will have the approximate temperature in Fahrenheit degrees. Holy cricket!

How to deal with biting bugs

One unfortunate side effect of being outside is getting bit by bugs. The worst offenders are ticks and mosquitoes. For ticks there are a few things to do to avoid getting a bite, which is really the most important step.

→ Wear light-colored clothing so it is easier to spot ticks on you.
→ Tuck your pants into your socks so ticks can't crawl in.
→ Spray yourself and your clothing with insect repellent.
→ Wash all of your clothes when you get home.
→ Do a thorough tick check when you get home, including belly button, behind your knees and ears, arm pits, groin, and, of course, hair.

Mosquitoes

Sadly, mosquitoes actually prefer to munch on juicy little children than adults. You are so much sweeter! The fact is, you will most likely get bit many times by mosquitoes and it will itch, but the trick is not to scratch it. My grandmother taught me to take my fingernail and make an x through the bite, then rub a paste of baking soda and water over it. You can also put ice on bites to help the swelling, as well as calamine lotion or hydrocortisone. Whatever happens, don't let a few bad bugs ruin your outside adventures.

NATURE SCAVENGER HUNT

A nature scavenger hunt is one of my favorite ways to spend the day because it includes gathering, scavenging, and exploring all in one. There are lots of ways to have a good hunt, but basically you need a list of things to look for. The following are some of the things that are fun to find, but remember, the list can go on and on.

Find:
- [ ] Something thin
- [ ] Something smooth
- [ ] Something round
- [ ] Something green, blue, red, etc.
- [ ] Something that is shaped like "Y"
- [ ] Something rough
- [ ] Something twisted
- [ ] Something see-through
- [ ] Something fragile
- [ ] Something that can be tied

If you are in your backyard, you can gather some of your finds and bring them in to use for the following art projects. But do not pick live plants or gather materials from parks and public areas. Nature in these places is for all of us to admire.

FLOWER/LEAF PRESS

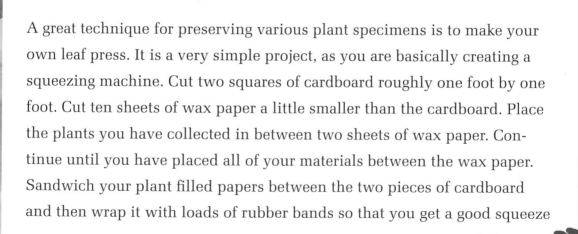

Materials:

Thick cardboard

Wax paper

Plant specimens

Rubber bands

A great technique for preserving various plant specimens is to make your own leaf press. It is a very simple project, as you are basically creating a squeezing machine. Cut two squares of cardboard roughly one foot by one foot. Cut ten sheets of wax paper a little smaller than the cardboard. Place the plants you have collected in between two sheets of wax paper. Continue until you have placed all of your materials between the wax paper. Sandwich your plant filled papers between the two pieces of cardboard and then wrap it with loads of rubber bands so that you get a good squeeze effect. Wait several weeks before uncovering your plants. When you remove the rubber bands, you should have nice, flat plants and flowers to use in your journal or art projects.

CONTACT PAPER COLLAGE

This is another way to preserve your collections and make a lovely sun catcher while you are at it. Buy clear contact paper at any home goods store. After a nice round of scavenging, peel off the backing of a piece of contact paper and tape the outer edge on a flat surface, so that the sticky side is up and ready for things to be stuck to it. Arrange your collections the way you want them and then put another piece of contact paper over them. You can seal the edges with colorful washi or duct tape and punch some holes in the top to hang in your window. As the sun shines through, you will be reminded of the day's adventure!

DANDELION CHAINS

The great thing about making dandelion chains is that in the summer no one ever minds if you pick a dandelion from their yards because, boy, are they plentiful! Another great perk to wearing a dandelion chain in the summer is that it will keep away mischievous fairies, allowing you to look festive without being bothered by fairy trouble. Scour the yard for dandelions with very thick and long stems. Using your fingernail, slice a one inch tear through the stem. Thread the stem of another dandelion through this hole. Then take your fingernail and slice through this next dandelion stem. Continue until your chain is the length for a crown or a necklace. Or you can go for the dandelion chain world record like my daughters do each summer.

BUG HUNTS

Although it is hard to do—especially when the mosquitoes or black flies are biting—we sometimes forget about the very smallest among us for the very reason that they are so tiny. We share the world with millions and millions of creepy crawlies and it only takes a couple of minutes in the woods

to see them. Insects are everywhere, but the best way to start finding them is to imagine being small. Look under things and listen for their tiny movements. Wait patiently and surely a bug will cross your path. Use your notebook and jot down the different types that you see. Carefully lift logs and see the roly polies and centipedes underneath. Then gently place the log back the way it was. You can also put a white sheet out in a buggy area and see how many bugs crawl over it. Have a magnifying glass ready and then help that little friend back to a leafy hideaway.

MOTH MADNESS

During the summer, moths flock to light and although they can be a bit of a bother, moths can have beautiful wings like their butterfly relations. For an easy and moth-friendly attraction method, you can hang a white cloth under a bright light. If you have a clothesline, use that to hang a white sheet and bring out a lantern and flashlights. Place the light sources in front of the sheets and wait a few seconds before you are a moth motel. Look with your flashlights at all the different types of moths that have checked in. You can even have a moth guide book nearby to find out their names.

BIRD WATCHING

You have no doubt noticed the birds that flock to your feeder or your yard. Perhaps a certain bossy blue jay likes to dominate the area, or maybe a gentler wren visits each day. Perhaps eagles circle above your house checking out your cat. But with more than 926 species of birds in North America, there are quite a few more feathered friends than you might think from just surveying your yard. The best way to begin the art of bird watching is to get hold of a guide book. *The Sibley Guide to Birds* is a great one to start with, but there are also more specific guides to each region. Binoculars help you see those birds that are far away in the trees, but identifying with your naked eyes is a good first step in this hobby. Also, you'll want your journal to record your various sightings.

When identifying a bird, here are a few things to look for:

✔ The overall shape and size of the bird and whether there is anything unusual about the shape of the bird's wings, beak, or feet.

✔ Any special markings or colors on the bird.

✔   Where are you when you see the bird—by the ocean, in the woods, in your back yard, or in the mountains? This will determine the bird's habitat.

✔   Can you hear its bird song? (We will talk more about this in a minute.)

As you begin this pursuit, there are a couple of very important rules. Do not disturb birds that are nesting or any eggs in a nest and never bring your dog or cat with you as you bird watch!

3 WAYS TO HELP THE BIRDS

Feeders:

Helping a bird with a little extra snack is a great thing to do. You can make simple birdfeeders from pinecones slathered with peanut butter or shortening and coated with bird seed or purchase elaborate feeders from stores. Just know that different birds like different kinds of food—just like you and your parents.

- ✔ Woodpeckers like suet

- ✔ Finches, cardinals, nuthatches, and chickadees like black oil sunflower seeds

- ✔ Indigo bunting prefer millet

- ✔ Goldfinches are fond of thistle seed

Houses:

A simple wooden birdhouse can offer a safe haven for a bird to roost. Not all birds will flock to your birdhouse but enough species do enjoy the safety it provides to make it worth your time. Basic birdhouses and kits are readily available but it need not be complex, as I have heard of birds nesting in the half shell of a coconut. Providing nesting material is another

lovely gift to the birds. They adore anything soft and stringy to pad their beds. Dryer lint, fine wood chips, wool, and string are all nesting favorites.

Baths:

Believe it or not, birds actually like bathing, unlike some of you. Making a quick bird bath is a surefire way to get birds to visit your yard. They will not only clean themselves but the bath provides a good spot for them to have a quick drink. But make sure to keep the water fresh. Before you know it you will be attracting mosquitoes not birds! The simplest bird bath to make is to turn a terracotta planter upside down. Then place the large saucer on top. Fill with water and the birds can scrub-a-dub.

BIRD CALLS

Rachel Carson called the bird song around us "the bird chorus," and to be able to appreciate the variety of their songs is something worthy of the hours it takes to learn to recognize them. A nice trick is that some birds are named for their calls, like "chick-a-dee-dee" for chickadee and the phoebe, which says, "fee-bee". The American robin says "cheerily, cheer-up, cheer-ily," and barred owls say "who cooks for you?" Listen to the songs around you in the spring and summer and see what they sound like to you. Learn these calls and then you can learn the names of the birds. A great resource

No child should grow up unaware of the dawn chorus of the birds in spring. He will never forget the experience of a specially planned early rising and going out in the predawn darkness. The first voices are heard before daybreak. It is easy to pick out these first solitary singers. Perhaps a few cardinals are uttering their clear, rising whistles, like someone calling a dog. Then the song of a white throat, pure and ethereal, with the dreamy quality of remembered joy. Off in some distant patch of woods a whippoorwill continues his monotonous night chant, rhythmic and insistent, sound that is felt almost more than heard. Robins, thrushes, song sparrows, jays, vireos add their voices. The chorus picks up volume as more and more robins join in, contributing a fierce rhythm of their own that soon becomes dominant in the wild medley of voices. In that dawn chorus one hears the throb of life itself.

● Rachel Carson

is the website for the Cornell Lab of Ornithology, which has audio clips of thousands of birds. Create your own unique call and try talking to the birds around you. Who knows, maybe they will understand you better than some of the people in your life do.

Night Tree

Eve Bunting wrote a magical book called **The Night Tree** about a family who head to the woods every year before Christmas to decorate a tree with food for the animals. They cover this particular tree with berries and seed, carrots and apples. It is their way of celebrating the holidays with nature and giving back to the animals around them. Creating your own night tree celebration is not only a great family activity, but it can help the animals in winter. First, find a tree in your backyard or deep in the woods nearby. Prior to the night you decorate, spend time preparing the edible ornaments. You can create lots of animal friendly decorations, such as strings of cheerios, dried apples, carrots with holes hammered in the tops to thread string through, and bird-seed cookies. When you decorate your night tree, make sure to bring lanterns and warm clothing. Once you have hung up your ornaments, come back to see if the animals have eaten anything and look for tracks around your tree.

Amelia ~ A deer by the night tree

Bird-Seed Cookie Recipe

Mix one packet of pectin with two cups of cold water and bring to a boil, stirring frequently.

In a large bowl, mix one cup of flour with three cups of bird seed. Add liquid mixture and stir.

Fill mini muffin tins with mixture, or form balls by hand. Cut straws into two-inch pieces and then poke into the center of the cookie. This will allow a hole to set in the cookies so you can string a piece of yarn later.

Let the cookies set for about six hours before removing them from the muffin tray. Depending on how dry they are when you pull them out, you might need to turn them upside down and allow them to set on the underside as well.

Tie a string or piece of yarn through the hole and hang them on a tree for our animal friends to enjoy during the winter.

ANIMAL TRACKS

Identifying animal tracks is a surefire way to know what kind of animal neighbors you have, whether they are squirrels, pigeons, or more wild creatures like deer or fox. Basically, animal tracks are another way of saying footprints. Just as when you walk on the beach or through snow you leave tracks, so do animals as they roam the woods and even your neighborhood. Finding and identifying animal tracks is like being a nature detective, following clues and looking closely at evidence. The easiest way to see animal tracks is when it snows, but you can just as easily find them in the mud or soft dirt. Early morning light is the best for spotting fresh tracks plus many animals are the busiest at night. Once you find a set of tracks, follow it to see where the animal went. Sometimes small animals are able to get into much tighter spots than you can, but it is still worth a try.

You will need to familiarize yourself with the different tracks before you set out on a hunt. Depending on how an animal walks will determine the type of track they make. There are four major kinds of track patterns. The first kind are hoppers like squirrels, mice, and rabbits, who have five toes on their back feet and four toes on their front feet.

The second are walkers, like deer and fox that walk on skinny legs. Bounders are another kind of track, and skunks do this by placing their front feet next to each other as well as their back feet, then leaping so that

their back feet fall in same spot. Last come the waddlers, such as raccoons and beavers. These animals put their hind feet next to their front feet and waddle along.

So the tracks will vary depending on the animal's movements. If you find a really interesting track you can create a cast of it with some plaster of Paris and a small picture frame. You frame the track, add water to your plaster and pour it over the track. After about twenty minutes you will be able to pull up the plaster and find the track imprinted in your mold.

By studying tracks, you will be able to understand the wildlife in your backyard: Which cats came in and did they chase any mice? Did a deer come in and eat your mom's favorite flowers? How about a skunk who keeps stinking things up? This is a very good way of being a nature detective and following the clues left by the animals around us.

CLOUD WATCHING

There is nothing quite like the lazy day feeling of watching clouds as they scuttle past. One of my most favorite pastimes is to try to find objects in the clouds. We have found unicorns, bears, sail boats, alligators, dinosaurs, and even entire villages chased by giants. Learning about the clouds can make you feel, as my daughter says, like a fortune teller. You know what the weather is going to do without having to watch any weather stations. The major cloud formations are as follows:

Stratus: The flat, grey ones you see before rain. These clouds usually fill the sky completely and they vary from dark gray to white.

Cirrus: They are very high and wispy clouds and seeing them means there is a lot of wind in the upper atmosphere, so it is likely that a change of weather is coming.

Cumulus: The fluffy popcorn clouds. They appear on sunny days and are known for fair weather.

Cumulusnimbus: These are large, dramatic cumulus clouds with high cottony towers. They usually mean a thunderstorm is coming.

Mackerel Clouds: These are also known as "school of fish" clouds. They are a low lumpy layer of cloud.

ONE FINAL ACT

So after all of these activities, what else could there be? You have gotten out there and given those boots a good mudding. I see grass stains and notebooks full of observations. I see red cheeks and smell the fresh air wafting off of you. "Good on ya," as they say in Australia and New Zealand. But there is one last task. The earth has shared itself readily with you. Given you dirt, rocks, sticks, and water. It has let you watch the clouds, track animals, and listen to birds and bugs, and only a few have bitten you! Now it is time for you to adopt a piece of the planet. This sounds harder than it is. No papers need to be filed. You don't need to bring a piece of the

earth home and give it a place on your bed. All you need to do is find some patch of earth that could use a little help. Maybe it is a park in your town that no one goes to anymore and it is piled up with litter. Maybe it is a bare spot in your own yard that could use some flowers to attract birds and bees. Maybe you can bring some bird feeders to an elderly person's home and help keep them filled. You can just continue getting your boots muddy by digging in the dirt a bit more. Plant some trees in exchange for the paper you use. Plant some bushes to make a habitat for small animals like squirrels and birds. Plant some grass or seedlings to bring a bare patch of soil back to health. And then tell all of your friends. Share your stories of mud and sticks. Bring them out to see your forts. Listen to bird songs together. Watch the path of the sun to tell time. Count the chirps of crickets to determine how hot it is. Pay attention together. You are the ones who will make this planet stay muddy and wonderful.

BOOKS TO CONTINUE THE ROMP...

A Kid's Guide to Building Forts by Tom Birdseye and illustrated by Bill Klein

Andrew Henry's Meadow by Doris Burn

Earth Child: Early Science for Young Children by Kathryn Sheehan and
Mary Waidner

Honeysuckle Sipping: The Plant Lore of Childhood by Jeanne R. Chesanow

*I Love Dirt: 52 Activities to Help You and Your Kids Discover the Wonders of
Nature* by Jennifer Ward

Kid's Camp! Activities for the Backyard or Wilderness by Laurie Carlson and
Judith Dammel

*Nature's Playground: Activities, Crafts, and Games to Encourage Children to
Get Outside* by Fiona Danks and Jo Schofield

Nature Smart: Awesome Projects to Make with Mother Nature's Help by
Gwen Diehn, Terry Krautwurst, Allan Anderson, Joe Rhatigan, and
Heather Smith

Mud Pies and Other Recipes by Marjorie Winslow

Night Tree by Eve Bunting and illustrated by Ted Rand

Roxaboxen by Alice McLerran and illustrated by Barbara Cooney

Seed Bombs: Going Wild with Flowers by Josie Jeffery

Summer: A User's Guide by Suzanne Brown

Sunflower House by Eve Bunting

Sunflower Houses: Inspiration from the Garden: A Book for Children and their Grown-ups by Sharon Lovejoy

The Sense of Wonder by Rachel Carson

The Stick Book: Loads of Things You Can Make or Do with a Stick by Fiona Danks and Jo Schofield

Wonderful Houses around the World by Yoshio Komatsu

Woods Walk by Henry Art

ACKNOWLEDGMENTS

after a good chunk of time on this planet, I am still awed by the world outside my door. Writing this book was a small tribute to the great big magical world we live in. Rachel Carson was my muse, as her transformative essay "A Sense of Wonder" provided a backbone to this book and has informed my life's work with children and nature. As much awe as I hold for nature, books come in at a close second, so writing one about adventures outside was a sweet spot in my life. Thank you to Michael Steere for taking this idea and letting me run with it, even though I sometimes got a little stuck in the mud. Lynda Chilton always takes my words and brings them to life with her vibrant designs and incredible eye. Thank you to all the people who work so hard to bring the book to the people, especially Linda Callahan and Terry Bregy, for whom I am truly grateful.

I am lucky to be involved with some truly special places where kids can create and explore. Sweet Tree Arts in Hope, Maine, allowed me to experiment with muddy messes and get more than boots dirty. Thank you Lindsay Pinchbeck for all that you do and bring to our community. Thank

you to Peopleplace Cooperative Preschool for letting the kids lead and making sure it is always artistic, messy, and, most important, joyful. And thank you for documenting it along the way so we could include the evidence in this book!

I am so thankful to live in a place that is chock full of outdoor activities and incredible vistas. Thank you to the people in this community—who do most of these activities on a daily basis—for the inspiration, and for sharing stories, photographs, and your kids with me.

I wouldn't love the dirt as much if my childhood hadn't been so filled with outside time. Thank you to my parents for letting us explore freely and for giving us such a great neighborhood to romp around. Thank you to my brother for encouraging me to wear pants and ride dirt bikes. I am especially thankful to my daughters, Phoebe and Daphne, who make the world a better place and also willingly try out everything and are constantly giving me new and better ideas. Their forts are second to none, not to mention their mud pies. And thank you, ultimately to Jeff, for keeping us all moving through the muddy patches with ease, laughter, and patience.